JB

Marvin

Ortisé

Aston

WE LOVE JLS

By Sarah Palmer

Published 2012.

Pedigree Books Limited, Beech Hill House,
Walnut Gardens, Exeter, Devon EX4 4DH

www.pedigreebooks.com | books@pedigreegroup.co.uk

All images courtesy of Rex Features

ISBN 9781907602771

£7.99

Contents

JB

Name Jonathan Benjamin Gill

Date of birth 07/12/1986

Starsign Sagittarius

From Croydon

Lives London

Nicknames Gilly, Gillster, JG, JB

Siblings One brother called Neequaye Gill

Eye colour Brown

Height 5' 6"

Shoe size Nine

Pets None

Phobias Snakes

Favourite film Bad Boys II

Favourite colour Yellow

Favourite food Chinese

Favourite TV show He loves documentaries

Favourite sports Rugby, football

Favourite subject at school Japanese!

Celeb crushes Megan Fox

Instruments he can play Flute, piano and guitar

Hidden talents JB is a qualified diver and a budding chef

First album bought The Backstreet Boys' Backstreet's Back

Marvin

FACT FILE

Marvin

Name Marvin Richard James Humes

Date of birth 18/03/1985

Starsign: Pisces

From Greenwich, London

Lives London

Nicknames Marv

Siblings Two brothers – Jackson who is younger and Leon who is older.

Eye colour Brown

Height 6' 0"

Shoe size Nine

Pets None

Phobias Tarantulas

Favourite films Moonwalker, Armageddon, Goonies and the Back To The Future trilogy

Favourite colour Green

Favourite food Nando's

Favourite TV show The Simpsons

Favourite sports Football, golf

Favourite subject at school Business Studies

Celeb crushes Pamela Anderson, Cheryl Cole and, er, Rochelle Wiseman

Instruments he can play Piano

First album bought Michael Jackson's Bad

FACT FILE

Ortisé

Name Oritsé Jolomi Matthew Soloman Williams

Date of birth 27/11/1986

Starsign Sagittarius

From Shepherds Bush, London

Lives London

Nicknames Glitzy Ritzy, Music Boy, Barrack, 'Ritsé

Siblings Oritsé has two brothers and one sister

Eye colour Hazel

Height 5' 6"

Shoe size Nine and a half

Pets He had a gerbil when he was 11

Phobias Vertical theme park rides

Favourite film The Shawshank Redemption

Favourite colour Red

Favourite food Nando's

Favourite TV show Family Guy

Favourite sports Table tennis

Favourite subject at school Poetry and English

Celeb crushes Mariah Carey, Rihanna and Eva Longoria

Instruments he can play Guitar

Hidden talents Oritsé formed JLS!

Aston

Aston

Name Aston Iain James Merrygold

Date of Birth 13/02/1988

Starsign Aquarius

From Peterborough

Lives London

Nicknames Lil Man, A.S

Siblings Aston has four younger brothers called Kane, Anthony, Reece and Ashley, plus a half-brother, Connor and half-sister, Courtney

Eye colour Brown

Height 5' 5"

Shoe size Eight and a half

Pets None

Phobias Big dogs!

Favourite film The Pursuit Of Happyness

Favourite colour Blue

Favourite food Pizza

Favourite TV show The Simpsons

Favourite sports Football

Favourite subjects at school P.E. and Drama

Celeb Crushes The Olsen Twins, Cheryl Cole, Vanessa Hudgens, Ashley Tisdale and Hayden Pannetiere

Instruments he can play None

Hidden talents Acting

First album bought Usher's My Way

The boys had all been doing their own thing until fate bought them together

RISE TO FAME

They're talented, successful and have massive hopes for the future. This is JLS's story so far...

The members of JLS already had a solid background in performing before forming the band. Oritsé had been doing an internship at a record company and competing in talent competitions since he was 14, Marvin had appeared in several TV shows and been part of the girl/boy band VS, Aston had worked as a kids' TV presenter and dabbled in acting, while JB had been singing from a young age.

It had long been Oritsé's dream to form a UK version of hit American R&B band Boyz II Men, and when he met Marvin through friends, things started to slot into place.

When Marvin later met Aston at an audition for a TV ad, he knew he would make the perfect addition to the group. But it was only when they met JB at the 2007 X Factor auditions that the gang was complete.

The lads soon bonded and started working on music under the name UFO. They released a mash up of Sean Kingston's Beautiful Girls and Ben E King's Motown classic Stand By Me, and the single went on to win them the Best Unsigned Act gong at the Urban Music Awards.

They released one more single as UFO, Slap Ya Elbow, before deciding to take things to the next level.

In 2008, having grown in confidence hugely, they felt ready to try out for the fifth series of The X Factor in a bid to win the £1 million record deal.

They were an instant hit with the judges and became firm favourites to win. However, when the all-important final rolled around, sadly they were pipped to the post by Alexandra Burke.

But all was not lost and they were soon offered a record deal by music giant Epic, and the guys set about creating their debut album.

Their first single, Beat Again, was a No. 1 smash when it was released in July 2009. The follow up, Everybody In Love, followed suit, and their self-titled album also hit the top spot when it was released in November 2009. The band had well and truly arrived.

Three years on they're one of the biggest bands in the UK and are known for their incredible live shows.

They've raised loads of money for charity, released their own hit documentary, JLS: Eyes Wide Open 3D, and were even invited to perform at the Queen's Diamond Jubilee Concert in June 2012.

With so much success already behind them, what does the future hold for these super-talented guys? Only time will tell, but we predict more amazing things to come!

Their live shows were honed during The X Factor

At yet another award ceremony. This time, the MOBOs

Like the signs say;
"We Love JLS!"

LIVE!

1 The lads' concerts are always massive sellers

2 All of the boys say touring is on of their fave things to do

3 Aston loves showing off his acrobatic skills on stage

4 JLS's shows are always full of surprises

5 The guys love doing cover versions of their fave tracks!

Award winners

They're so brilliant we're not surprised
JLS have won so many top awards

2007
Urban Music Awards – Best Unsigned Act

2009
MOBO Awards – Best Newcomer

2010
MOBO Awards – Best UK Act, Best Album for JLS, Best Song for Beat Again

BRITs – British Breakthrough Act, British Single for Beat Again

BBC Switch Live Awards – Switch's Outstanding Artist

BT Digital Music Awards – Best Group, Best Video for Everybody In Love

Urban Music Awards – Best Group, Best R&B Act

2011
BT Digital Music Awards – Best Video for Eyes Wide Shut

DID YOU KNOW?

Sit back and enjoy this fine selection of random JLS facts!

1 When Aston was 14 he appeared on Stars In Their Eyes as Michael Jackson and sang Rockin' Robin.

2 Radio 1's Trevor Nelson heard Oritsé sing when he was younger and asked him to perform one of his own songs on his MTV show The Lick.

3 Before auditioning for The X Factor, JB was studying Theology at King's College in London.

4 Oritsé wrote the song Wow Oh Wow for Jedward.

5 Aston had his first kiss with a girl at a zoo! How very, er, romantic.

6 JB has two scars – one above his left eye and one on his chin.

7 JB lived in Antigua for five years before he moved to the UK.

8 Oritsé got his first break in the music industry by working for free for a record company called Deal Records.

9 Marvin's grandparents are Scottish, English and Jamaican.

10 While Marvin was still at school he appeared in the TV programmes Holby City and Grange Hill.

11 Aston originally wanted to be a professional football player.

12 Before trying out for The X Factor, Aston auditioned for a part in TV show Britannia High and made it to the final 16.

13 JB was a keen rugby player in school, and was apparently very good!

14 Aston reckons his worst habit is having too much energy.

15 The lads have a record deal in America and plan to launch themselves over there.

16 If JB has to be any animal, it would be a koala.

17 Marvin once slipped over on stage at Wembley Stadium in front of 80,000 people. Eek!

18 Oritsé's favourite quote is 'Victory After Victory'.

19 JB thinks his feet have shrunk as he's got older. Weird!

20 Their original name, UFO, stands for Unique Famous Outrageous.

COOL QUOTES

JLS have never been quiet about having their say. Here are some of our fave quotes from the lads!

JB

"We have a rule in the studio that anything goes. We thought we'd write up-tempo songs, down-tempo songs, happy songs, sad songs, love songs, inspirational songs, songs about our 3D movie…"

"When we are out as a group we have security with us, but individually we have to be careful. Sometimes it's easier to jump on the bus or tube – and we would like to do it but it isn't always possible. It's all part and parcel of the job though."

"We try not to take too much of everything in because you don't want to start believing your own hype."

"It's fantastic to see how many people are supporting us hoping for us to do well. We've been on tour, so we get screaming fans every day. Although crying always gets to us – we never know whether they're happy or sad."

"You guys support us at any cost and we love you for it."

"I like clever girls, but they don't have to be into music."

"I spend the longest in the shower. Marvin spends the most time with skincare. Oritsé has to look in the mirror at least 100 times."

"If I had to put my finger on it I think people can see the genuine bond we have between us."

"We genuinely are best friends and genuinely love what we do and that's something you can't manufacture. It's real."

"We're still a young band with a lot to prove."

"Anybody who is anybody can listen to JLS and enjoy us. We'll cater to anybody who shows a desire to listen."

"People always say we're working too hard, but we're constantly writing all the time for fun. We write together, individually and in pairs so it means we often get a lot of material together very quickly."

"What we do can be lonely, you get so many girls screaming at you and then you go back to your hotel at night and wind up in bed alone."

"I'm really particular with hands and feet. You can tell a lot about a woman by the way she looks after them."

Marvin

"My role models are first and foremost, I think, my parents. My mum and dad have been great role models to me. The fact that they are still together. They have been married over 25 years which is inspirational."

"We all can't wait to be dads."

"I always used to steal my dad's aftershave when I was at school. I remember one time he caught me because he was off sick. Everyday I'd put on his Fahrenheit or CK One. And not just one or two sprays!"

Ortisé

"I don't see a problem with dating a fan at all."

"When we first got together we wrote a list of over 300 things we wanted to achieve and every time we met up to rehearse we would go through it and focus on what we would accomplish that week."

"The best thing about being in JLS is definitely doing what I love every single day whether it be performing, song writing or meeting fans."

"I want the whole planet to turn blue, green, yellow and red. JLS will be the government and everyone, like the police, will have JLS T-shirts as part of their uniform."

"We went through some of the toughest times when we first started out together, struggling, trying to get by and keep the band flying and that has given us our foundation. If the foundation is strong the house won't fall down."

"The creative process for us is one of the most fun and exciting times. Songs are a great outlet – to have the opportunity to get things off your chest like that."

"I do spend the most time in the mirror, but I'm always ready first."

"Blood couldn't make us (the band) closer."

"If you slip or slack, there's always gonna be someone behind you."

"To be honest we try not to think about the fame because then you get above your station."

"Me and Oritsé once got chased. It was lunchtime so we thought everyone would be in school. This bus full of girls went past, they saw us, started screaming and got off. That was it. We ran around the corner and there was an even bigger herd waiting for us."

"It's best to try not to get sucked into the hype too much. It's about the music and everything else is a bonus."

"Success depends on who you are and what dreams you have, for us, every time we release a single, success is to be able to celebrate that, no matter where it gets to."

"I never feel lonely in hotels. I'm a party animal who's always saying, 'Let's go out!' So when I'm in my hotel room, I just want to sleep!"

Aston

IT'S WRITTEN IN THE STARS

We reveal what the boys' star signs say about them, from romance, to work, to friendships — the lot!

Aston: Aquarius

Two of the best qualities Aquarians have are their ability to be totally honest and loyal. They adore their friends and family and love spending time with them, but they're also very independent and like time on their own. They always like to be one step ahead and know what's around the corner. They're not big fans of surprises!

Career-wise they suit a wide range of occupations and would be great doing something where they have to use their brains. However, their creative edge means they're also drawn to the arts and entertainment side of things, so Aston is definitely in the right job.

Aquarians like being in love and they're caring and loving and willing to sacrifice everything to make a relationship work. But it's not all good news — they can be demanding and needy and have very high standards, so you need to be strong to handle them!

Oritsé and JB: Sagittarius

Sagittarians are open-minded and friendly, and they're also known to be trustworthy. Their mates can always rely on them to help out when they're in trouble, and because they think in a very straightforward way, they're great at giving advice.

Sagittarians are unpredictable and they can change their mind about something from one minute to the next. However, this also means they aren't afraid to try something new. Their upfront manner means they would make great teachers or personal trainers.

When it comes to romance, they are very black and white so you'll always know where you stand with them. They're passionate and kind, but they hate to feel like they're being put under pressure, so anyone who goes out with them needs to give them their own space to express themselves.

Marvin: Pisces

Pisceans are known for their generous nature, so if you have one as a friend you can expect to get some nice presents on your birthday! They have a very sensitive side and they're intuitive so they always make good decisions when it comes to making new friends. It may take a while to get to know them, but once you do you've got a mate for life.

They're just as giving when it comes to romance and always want to take care of their partner and make sure they feel loved. They can be very romantic when they're in the mood and like their partner to feel cared for. However, they do expect a lot in return, so if you date a Piscean you need to be very attentive and make sure they know how great you think they are.

When it comes to their career they love doing anything that's creative – hence being a pop star is the perfect occupation for Marvin!

FAMOUS FANS

The fun-loving foursome have been gaining their own celeb following since their X-Factor days

KATE MOSS Marvin revealed that supermodel Kate went backstage after a show and was asking after JB. "JB's real name is Jonathan. She came over to us and was, like, 'Where's Jonathan?' because he wasn't with us."

DAME JUDI DENCH The legendary actress contacted JLS back in 2009 and claimed her and her family were "huge fans". Oritsé said he was "blown away by it all".

ONE DIRECTION You might think these lads would be rivals, but actually you're more likely to see the two bands hugging it out. Harry Styles has said of JLS, "They really look out for us."

SIMON COWELL Si is very proud that JLS have done so well and says, "They're hard working, they respect their fans, and they're super, super talented."

ROBBIE WILLIAMS Marvin has called Robbie "an inspiration", and when JLS were recording in LA he invited them to play on his 5-a-side footie team and even did some JLS dance moves when he scored!

USHER JLS have a huge superstar fan in the form of Usher. He recently met them at his album showcase and said that he loved their sound. Oritsé has also revealed that he has written a song for US singer.

These Are A Few Of Their
Favourite Things!

What do Tina Turner and Vivienne Westwood have in common? Here's what JLS like the most...

JB loves...

Cars. But mainly his Mercedes E-class coupé which he has referred to as 'the love of my life'.

A good bum. He admits it's the first thing he checks out when he meets a girl!

Rugby. Until he was 18 he was regularly playing for a team and nearly pursued it professionally.

Nando's. He once ate a whole chicken (plus sides) in one sitting!

Burberry. He's a big fan of the swanky designer clothing range.

The Script. He's always got the Irish rockers on his iPod ready to go.

RUGBY

THE CARIBBEAN

The Caribbean. Like Oritsé, it's his number one holiday destination.

'If' by Rudyard Kipling. It's his favourite poem ever.

Prince. He says the superstar's concert is the best he's ever been to.

PRINCE

THAILAND

PAMELA ANDERSON

Marvin loves...

Thailand. It's his favourite place to jet off to when he needs to relax.

Vivienne Westwood. He reckons the designer clobber is perfect for his 'look'.

Las Vegas. He's a big fan, which is why he chose to go there for his stag do.

Golf. He loves a game with his pals when the band have time off.

Michael Jackson. His Bad tour was the first concert he ever saw and he's always been a huge fan.

Pamela Anderson. The actress was his first ever crush.

Chelsea FC. He often clashes with Aston about this!

Rochelle Wiseman. He's never stops talking about the love of his life.

Beyoncé. He listens to her music all the time.

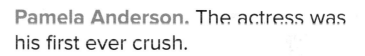

BEYONCÉ

Eddie Murphy. His stand-up especially.

TINA TURNER

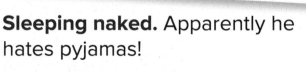

THE CARIBBEAN

Oritsé loves...

Songwriting. He started at a young age and still writes constantly now.

The Lion King. It makes him cry!

N.E.R.D. He's always wanted to meet frontman Pharrell Williams.

The Caribbean. It's his absolute favourite holiday destination.

Tina Turner. Oritsé went to see the legendary singer in concert and was blown away.

Sleeping naked. Apparently he hates pyjamas!

Ambition. He's always had massive dreams and wants JLS to become the biggest band in the world.

Camden Market. He loves finding hidden gems and clothes that other people haven't got so he can stand out from the crowd.

Cartoons. He admits to reading The Beano!

Aston loves...

Arsenal Football club. He hates it when he misses matches.

Fast cars. He's building a nice little collection including a white Audi R8 and a grey California Ferrari.

His mum. He says she's his best friend in the world. Awww.

Embarrassing his mates. He's the practical joker of the group.

Boyz II Men. It's been his top gig to date.

Partying. He says his ideal weekend is going out late, lying in and then hanging out with mates.

Will Smith. The actor and singer cracks him up.

America. He loves holidaying in the USA, especially Florida.

All Saints. He buys loads of clothes from the super-cool shop.

Tomato ketchup. He puts it on everything!

Tattoos. He's got loads, including a full sleeve.

ARSENAL FC

BOYZ II MEN

SMITH

TOMMY K

HEINZ 1869 TOMATO KETCHUP

WHY WE LOVE JLS

Just a few reasons why the lads are just so adorable!

They're still humble
Even though they're huge stars, the boys say they'll never be big-headed because they all make sure they keep each other's feet on the ground. They reckon if they did start to get big-headed, their mums would give them a slap!

They do loads of charity work
Having set up the JLS Foundation, the boys regularly visit hospitals and take part in fundraising activities. Their Sport Relief single, Proud, and their visit to Africa contributed to the £62m final amount raised in 2011. Actually amazing!

They keep their bods looking buff
JB says that the boys spend hours in the gym doing pull-ups and weights to look good for their fans. Luckily although their gym schedule is strict, they still make time for Nando's and pizza!

They love a good cry
One of Oritsé's fave films is The Lion King, which still brings tears to his eyes, whilst Aston says that the Pursuit Of Happyness made him cry more than he has done in years. Sniff.

They love treating their ladies
Marvin bought fiancée Rochelle a £50k Range Rover Sport and JB has splashed out on loads of five-star holidays for him and long-term girlfriend, Chloe. All the boys think that treating a woman like a princess is the best thing a man can do.

They grant wishes
When a very ill fan Tweeted the boys telling them it was her wish to meet and sing with them, they invited her along to perform with them on stage at a concert in London. Scream!

They're completely hyper
The boys have been told off on shoots and in interviews because they're easily distracted. They often start running around and jumping on things and love having a laugh with each other.

They think they have the best fans in the world
Aston once said that if he could, he would want to buy a plaque for all the JLS fans saying "We love you more". Meanwhile, Marvin says it's his dream for "every one of our JLSters to meet us". We'd be at the front of the queue!

They keep in touch with their fans
Oritsé has said communicating with the band's fans is the most important thing to him. He often direct messages the most devoted ones on Twitter to say thanks for their support.

They never get sick of each other
Even though they see each other every day, JLS never tire of each other. They still go on holiday together and all refer to each other as brothers. So cute!

Discography

JLS already have loads of hits under their belts, and we reckon this is just the beginning!

Singles

Beat Again – July 2009

Everybody In Love – November 2009

One Shot – February 2010

The Club Is Alive – July 2010

Love You More – November 2010

Eyes Wide Shut (Featuring Tinie Tempah) – February 2011

She Makes Me Wanna (Featuring Dev) – July 2011

Take A Chance On Me – November 2011

Eyes Wide Open – December 2011

Do You Feel What I Feel? – January 2012

Proud – March 2012

Albums

JLS – November 2009

Outta This World – November 2010

Jukebox – November 2011

PAPPED!

JLS are no strangers to the paps — they follow them all over the place!

The guys are pros at being papped — wherever they are

The boys are happy to be snapped with fans

Aston: "Yes Mum, I'm on my way."

She'll never wash that T-shirt again!

Hats off to Oritsé for his funny photo face

FAMOUS FRIENDS

Now only are JLS massively famous themselves, they've got loads of top celeb pals too!

JADE EWENS Aston and the Sugababe singer were romantically linked way back in 2009, but it turned out they're just mates and are still pals now.

OLLY MURS Olly and the JLS guys have been mates for years. He supported them on their 2011 tour and says if he had to collaborate with one group, his first choice would be JLS.

DIANA VICKERS
The lads met Diana on The X Factor, and she later supported them on some of their 2010 tour dates. The boys have said how proud they are she's done so well. Ahhh!

GIORGIO ARMANI The band went out for dinner with fancy designer Giorgio and his niece Roberta, and he even gifted the boys some suits. Oritsé later said, "Giorgio's the man."

THE WANTED People may assume the two bands are rivals, but they get on really well and catch up for a night out whenever they can fit it in.

ALICE COOPER American rocker Alice (ask your dad) bonded with the boys on the red carpet at an awards do, and asked to become the group's fifth member!

The gigantic JLS quiz

You're JLS's number one fan, right? Then you're sure to know the answers to these quezzas!

1 Which JLS boy is obsessed with tomato ketchup? *Aston*

2 Which band member supports Chelsea Football Club? *Marvin*

3 Which lad admits that The Lion King makes him cry? *oritse*

4 Who has a brother called Neequaye? *JB*

5 Which of the lads actually formed JLS? *oritse*

6 Whose favourite poem is If by Rudyard Kipling? *JB*

7 Who appeared in Holby City in their younger years? *Marvin*

8 Who admits to having a phobia of tarantulas? *Marvin*

9 What was the name of the Top Ten single the boys released in aid of Sport Relief? *Proud*

10 Who admits to reading classic comic The Beano? *Oritsei*

11 Whose top subject at school was Japanese? *JB*

12 Which band mate does Marvin say is the 'international wingman of the year'? *Oritse*

13 Which JLS guy hails from Peterborough? *Aston*

14 Who appeared on Stars In Their Eyes as Michael Jackson? *Aston*

15 Whose first crush was on actress Pamela Anderson? *Marvin*

16 Who claims their feet have shrunk as they've got older? *JB*

17 What was the name of the lads' first single? *Beat again*

18 Which JLS boy had their first kiss at a zoo? *Aston*

19 Who spends the most time in front of the mirror? *Oritsei*

20 Which guy once slipped over on stage at Wembley in front of 80,000 people?! *Marvin*

ANSWERS ON PAGE 77

JLS ON JLS

The boys know each other better than anyone, so what do they have to say about each other?

Aston on Marvin

"I don't really get much attention. Marvin gets the most as he's the oldest."

Aston on JB

"JB wakes up grumpy all the time! Don't talk to him in the morning."

Aston on Oritsé

"Oritsé is the hardest to wake up. He falls asleep anywhere. Like, we'll be in the car for five minutes, and he's asleep. It's a gift!"

Oritsé on the band

"We don't have a second to breathe. It's fantastic. We always said that when we got into this position we'd work as hard as we could. We are four of the most fortunate guys."

Marvin on Oritsé

"Oritsé is the international wingman of the year."

Oritsé on Marvin

"I think Marvin's the most sensible member of the band."

Aston on JB

"JB likes to stand next to a window, look up on the horizon and put lotion on himself."

JB on Aston

"Aston's the biggest hit with the ladies. He's the young cute one, isn't he?"

Oritsé onJB

"JB sucks his thumb!"

Marvin on the band

"We've achieved a lot and had the best start, but we want to keep our feet on the ground."

JB on the other lads
"The best thing about JLS is being able to travel all over the world with three of my top boys!"

JB on the guys
"We have individual styles that link up. Marv's the smartest, then me."

Aston on Oritsé
"He's got the thickest legs. He's got Beyoncé legs!"

Marvin on Oritsé
"Oritsé has got the craziest gym routine. He'll come back from a club and go to the gym."

Marvin on the band
"We're not having a break until we get to ten albums. Ten albums and ten tours."

Marvin on Aston
"Aston's pecs are much bigger than mine." (Jealous, eh?)

JB on Marvin
"He's always doing baby voices. He loves putting them on. He's got a little nephew, so he's always doing it."

Marvin on Oritsé
"He's a super lightweight. He only needs one glass of champagne and he'll dance the night away."

Aston on the boys
"It takes a minimum of two hours for everyone to be ready!"

I LOVE JLS BECAUSE...

What do you love most about JLS? Here's your chance to write down your fave things!

I love JLS because...

The moment I first started liking them was when... I was

My favourite member of JLS is... A Son

I think... AnSon is the best singer

The best JLS song is...

If I got to hang out with JLS I would like to...

The funniest thing I've heard about JLS is...

If I were to buy JLS something as a present, it would be...

If JLS were to buy me a present I would like it to be...

Of all of the guys... *A Ston* has the best style because...

If I got the chance to go on a date with one of the lads,
I would like... *A Ston* to take me to...

I really laughed when JLS...

The JLS member I'm most alike is... *a Ston* because...

I was shocked when I found out that JLS...

I really hope that JLS... *that JLS get back to gether.*

I would be the perfect fifth member of JLS because...

Spot the difference

Can you spot the five differences between these two pics of the boys?

ANSWERS ON PAGE 77

Quiz Answers

Are you a superfan or a superflop? Find out how well you did in our JLS quizzes!

Giant JLS quiz

1 Aston

2 Marvin

3 Oritsé

4 JB

5 Oritsé

6 JB

7 Marvin

8 Marvin

9 Proud

10 Oritsé

11 JB

12 Oritsé

13 Aston

14 Aston

15 Marvin

16 JB

17 Beat Again

18 Aston

19 Oritsé

20 Marvin

Spot the difference

1 JB's got a new tattoo

2 The logo on JB's T-shirt is missing

3 Oritsé's had a bit of a haircut

4 Ortisé's key chain has changed colour

5 Aston's missing his necklace